The Best of Life
by Ruth Heil

© of the German edition 1996,
Verlag der St.-Johannis-Druckerei, Lahr

© of the English translation 1996 Kevin Mayhew Ltd.

Published in Great Britain by
KEVIN MAYHEW LIMITED
Rattlesden, Bury St Edmunds
Suffolk IP30 0SZ
ISBN 0 86209 798 3
Cat. No. 1500047

Printed in Germany 1996

PICTURE CREDITS

Cover Picture: L. Bertrand

p.5 left: Bertrand Photographic Archives; p.5 right: R. Siegel; p.6: B. zur Bonsen;
p.7: P. Jacobs; p.8: M. Ruckszio; p.9: C. Palma; p.11 left: R. Haak; p.11 right: M. Ruckszio;
p.12: M. Will; p.13: L. Bertrand; p.14: M. Ruckszio; p.15: K. Radtke;
p.17 left: Kokta/IFA picture team; p.17 right: Lecom/IFA picture team; p.19: U. Kröner;
p.20: K. Radtke; p.21: M. Will; p.23 left: K. Radkte; p.23 right: R. Geitz; p.24: M. Ruckszio;
p.25: H. Mülnikel; p.27 left: L. Bertrand; p.27 right: P. Santor; p. 28: G. Hettler;
p. 29: H. Herfort; p.31 left: L.Lenz; p.31 right: P. Pönnighaus-Martin

FOREWORD

What do you think of first when you hear the word 'joy'?
  Do you think of freedom, adventure, success, sport, music, friends?
What gives you joy?
When does it grab you, hold you, satisfy you?
And when is it short-lived or soon forgotten, leaving just
    emptiness and pain?

Go with me on a journey to discover the true joy
    which keeps its promises.

Longing for Life

You are young and active, eager for life.
    Your expectations are boundless.
You want to be free; free to do what you like.
But you also realise that life means not only freedom,
    but restrictions;
    not only room to be yourself,
    but obligations to others.
So you have to find ways of making a success of life
    while recognising these limits.

Jesus says, 'Narrow is the gate that leads to life.'

Matthew 7:14

BUILDING A BRIDGE

Here is a bridge, begun but not complete.
It reaches far out towards what seems
unattainable.
You may have already built yourself
many bridges in your imagination,
though none of them ever brought you
to the land of your dreams.
But there is someone who will not only build you a bridge,
but *be* that bridge – the way to everlasting joy.

Jesus says, 'I am the way.' *John 14:6*

TURN TO THE SUN

The things which fill your days are the
things which will shape your life.

The people you spend your time with are the
ones who will influence you the most.

The voices you listen to
are those which will control you.

If you dabble with darkness,
  the darkness will overwhelm you;
  but if you let in the light,
  it will shine from within.

'You must live like people who belong to
  the light.' *Ephesians 5:8*

Be Patient

Everything worthwhile had a very small beginning.
Every plant which bears fruit started life as a tiny seed.
Don't give up on yourself.
Have the patience to wait.
Don't despair if you fail to fulfil your own expectations
or the dreams others have for you.
It is what *God* wants you to be which matters most of all.

'God created human beings in his own image.'

Genesis 1:27

Even Though you Stumble, Keep Climbing

Who doesn't want to leave their
troubles behind,
to soar into the air like a bird,
to hover among the clouds,
to be free?

But life keeps on dragging us down, holding us back.
The only way forward is to get up again and go on.

'Even the fittest may stumble and fall;
but those who look to the Lord . . . will soar on eagles' wings.'

Isaiah 40:30, 31

DON'T GIVE UP ON YOURSELF.
GOD HASN'T.

The beautiful butterfly began life as an
inconspicuous caterpillar,
inching its way up the tree
bit by bit.

But then it changed into a chrysalis,
which seemed like a living death,
until it broke free again
and spread its new found wings.

Now it could flutter easily from tree to tree,
light as a feather.

When you are feeling low and
    frustrated with your life,
    look at the butterfly,
    and learn that some things just take
    time, but they work out beautifully
    in the end.

'You need endurance in order to do
    God's will and win what he has
    promised.'   *Hebrews 10:36*

Reach for the Highest

If you are aiming for the very top, you know it is a
   challenge which will cost you something -
   the total commitment of your whole self.
But you know that the effort is worthwhile,
   because the goal is worthwhile.
The view from the mountain top is breathtaking.

And don't forget that other horizon -
   God's eternal kingdom.
That too is a spectacular vision
   worth total commitment.

'Set your mind on God's kingdom and his justice
   before everything else.'   *Matthew 6:33*

Stop and Ask the Way

Sometimes you feel you are missing something in life.
   You rush from one deadline to another,
      as if you are chasing your tail.
It is only when you look back that you realise
   you have lost your way.
That is the time to stop, and ask.
Don't be tempted to choose the paths that seem easy.
It isn't the speed you are travelling that matters,
   but the direction.

'You will show me the path of life.' *Psalm 16:11*

A LETTER FOR YOU

It's exciting to get letters,
whether it's a precious love letter,
news from distant friends or just
the latest catalogue.

Every letter has a purpose - to strengthen a relationship,
pass on information or sell a product.

And the Bible is a letter
    with a message for you.
It says you are loved.
It points you to God.
It offers you life.
Read it.

'Your word is a lamp to my feet, and a
    light to my path.' *Psalm 119:105*

TAKE TIME TO LOOK AROUND YOU

Observe the order and beauty in nature.
Look at the flowers by the path
and the beetle crawling through the grass.
Plants and animals thrive without any help from you,
and the smallest creature knows where to find food.
Discover in these things the wisdom of God
and learn to trust in him.

'Put all your trust in the Lord and do not rely
on your own understanding.
At every step you take keep him in mind,
and he will direct your path.' *Proverbs 3: 5, 6*

Beware!

Not everything can be recognised for what it is at first glance.

The spider's web becomes visible when the dew falls on it,
  and seems so beautiful and delicate.
But for the insect that gets caught in it,
  it becomes a deadly trap.

Do not be led astray by supposedly good
     friends, who whisper tempting words:
'Go on! Try it!'
'Everybody does it.'
'Once won't do you any harm.'
Recognise the trap before you get into it,
     and have the courage to keep clear.

'Stand up to the devil, and he will turn
     and run.' *James 4:7*

Wait for the Best

It is wonderful to be able to enjoy life,
  but even better to share it with someone else.
God places in every human being
  a deep longing for someone special.
Be prepared to wait for that someone,
  as you would want them to wait for you.
Do not be satisfied with the easy passing relationship
  which could harm both you and others.

'I have come that they may have life,
  and have it in all its fullness.' *John 10:10*

LEARN THE VALUE OF SILENCE

In the silence you hear those questions
    which are blotted out by noise.
Do not drown them out with loud music
    but learn the art of being still.

Listen for the inner voice
    which points out the way to life.
Give time to the needs of your spirit
    for it will outlive your body.

'When you seek me, you will find me; if you search with all your
    heart.' *Jeremiah 29:13*

Look Forward with Hope

Sometimes you may be filled with a sense of failure and despair.
    Your life seems as unpromising as ground
    which has been concreted over,
    in which nothing can grow or bloom.
But God has his own way of working.
He sometimes uses a bird to drop a tiny seed into a rusty grate;
    and from the depths there rises a surprise
    of new life bursting into flower.
That is God's destiny for you,
    if you let Jesus sow the seeds in your heart
    which will bring new colour into your life.

'In Christ Jesus the life-giving law of the Spirit has set you free
    from the law of sin and death.'   *Romans 8:2*

Learn Forgiveness

Understanding other people is sometimes hard work.
Our relationships become entangled and confused
even when we don't want them to.
Things are said and done which are afterwards regretted.
We hurt and are hurt.
We misunderstand and we are misunderstood.
The untangling begins when we are willing to accept
that we have not been hurt deliberately,
and we are ready to forgive
and be forgiven.

'You must forgive one another just as the Lord has
forgiven you.' *Ephesians 3:13*